The Swellest Wife Anyone Ever Had

The Swellest Wife Anyone Ever Had

Poems by

Jennifer Schomburg Kanke

© 2024 Jennifer Schomburg Kanke. All rights reserved.
This material may not be reproduced in any form, published,
reprinted, recorded, performed, broadcast,
rewritten, or redistributed without
the explicit permission of Jennifer Schomburg Kanke.
All such actions are strictly prohibited by law.

Cover design by Shay Culligan
Cover image by Vivienne Strauss
Author photo by Denise Wooley

ISBN: 978-1-63980-609-6

Kelsay Books
502 South 1040 East, A-119
American Fork, Utah 84003
Kelsaybooks.com

For all the grannies out there

Acknowledgments

Thank you to the following publications, in which versions of these poems previously appeared:

Arkana: "Not Understanding Palimpsests, She Thinks She Can Leave the Holler"
Change Seven: "Losing It"
The Dodge: "Confluence"
Eunoia Review: "Scenes from the Flood"
Gyroscope Review: "Chicken Fighting"
Hubris: "Scenes from the Flood"
Poetry Porch: "At the Tracy Park KIA-MIA Memorial"
Re-Verb: "That LeRoy's Such a Card"
River Heron Review: "Not Her Husband All Safe in His Grave"
SFPA Contest Winner: "The Prayer No One Said at Her Birth"
Spoon River Poetry Review: "Not Understanding Confinement, She Doesn't See the Big Deal About Shoes"
Women Speak: Women of Appalachia Project: "They'd Arrest You for That Now"

I would like to thank all of my friends and family who have made this book possible. Special thanks goes to my father and Aunt Jannie who shared so many stories with me; Denise, Geni, Jen, Brandi, Selena, Katie, Sherine, Lydia, Becca, Megan, and Wendy for all their support along the way; David Kirby, Barbara Hamby, Barry Faulk, Nick Mazza, Mark Halliday, Jill Rosser, Janis Butler Holm, Marge Piercy, and all the members of her intensive workshop in 2016, as well as Annie Finch and the Poetry Witch Community for your guidance and faith; Artemis, Hestia, and Aphrodite for always shining with their wild, homey, love; Tim, Ezzie, and Ellie for being by my side through it all; and Karen and everyone at Kelsay Books for helping bring this story into the world. May my work be seen by all who feel seen by my work.

Contents

First Love

Scioto County Boom Time	15
Will	16
Enid, Called Granny	17
The Prayer No One Said at Her Birth	18
They'd Arrest You for That Now	19
The Boy from the County Home	20
It Could Have Been Any Boy	21
The Mosquito	22
Enid Does the Work of Two	23
Scioto County Fair	24
Homecoming for the Ohio Council of Churches' Prince of Peace Declamation Contest Winner	25
While Others Enjoyed the Beggars Night Ball	26
Scenes from the Flood	27
Best Behave Now	35
If He Had Something	36
Marcescence After First Love	37
The Boy in the Dress Blues	38
How Easily She Broke the Thing	39
At the Tracy Park KIA-MIA Memorial	40

The Husband

Confluence	43
She Sets Her Sights on the Next Bright Boy	44
Another Beggars Night Ball	45
A Winter Walk	46
Guard	47
Natural Selection	48

Not Understanding Confinement,	
She Doesn't See the Big Deal About Shoes	49
Chicken Fighting	50
Mother-in-Law as False Prophet	51
Window Shopping	52
That LeRoy Is Such a Card	53
Priorities	54
Love Forever, LeRoy	55
Platoon 339 Leaves Camp Lejeune	
and Is One Step Closer to the Front	56
Sometimes Distraction Is the Only Hope There Is	57
Who Says That's Even What She's Looking For?	58
Quiet Secrets in Wartime	59
Traveling Light	60
That LeRoy Is Such a Card II	61
Packing Up	62
Homecoming	63
Not Caring the Color of His Heart,	
She Tries to Raise the Dead	64
Not Understanding Palimpsests,	
My Grandmother Thinks She Can	
Leave the Holler	65
Through the Blades	67
Bedtime Story	68
That LeRoy Is Such a Card III	69
Late Riser	70
Mama Says, If the Cancer Don't Kill Him,	
She Just Might	71
That LeRoy Is Such a Card IV	72
All the Wild Things Kept Inside	73
The Widow's Yoga	74
Not Her Husband All Safe in His Grave	75

Enid, Herself

She Knows What Counts	79
The Widow Takes a New Beau	80
Losing It	81
Hot Bath After Someone Else's Breakdown	82
Our Lord and Savior 4-F	84
It Wouldn't Have Changed a Thing	85
If It Ain't Broke	86
A Visit to Spalding County, Georgia	87
All the Women in My Family Have Singers But Me	88
Best Behave Now II	89
First Thanksgiving After Renovations	90
People Should Be at Home When It Rains	91
Hey There, Hornworm, Hawkmoth, or Whoever You Are	92
Granny at the Gallia Street Golden Corral	93
Granny, Called Enid	94

First Love

Scioto County Boom Time

There was the coke plant lit up through the night with its dull yellow sky from the
Benzene-packed air and its cancerous paychecks for veterans and farm boys.
One thousand jobs, they were lost in a year as the blast furnace shuttered its
doors and the open-hearth followed in time to make space for the vacuum.
Thirty percent of New Boston's school budget had turned into vapor as
Ivy-trained men were selling the land and equipment like nothing.
Then someone cleaned it enough for a Wal-Mart, for Oxy and pill mills,
singing loud hillbilly elegies just for political benefit.
See, too, the tourists getting away from Columbus through hollers of
chip and seal, gravel roads named for my people that lead to the
forests chartreuse with the riots of sassafras, oak, and young buckeyes.
Skimmers are feasting in slow moving creeks as the dragonfly naiads
head for the silt or what shelter they find in and under shale bridges or
limestone deposits, remains of the Ordovician boom times.

Will

Though I cannot carry the fires
of her hearth with me,
may this electric bill worn and yellow,
all these rusted pieces
of her ductwork, appease you. May this
pulsing in my stubborn
veins now bring you to me in my times
when my will is failing.
We are household, we are family.

Push the river to us, as the ocean's
not at hand right now.
Let me understand the creeks and
hills though concrete raised me,
as immovable as Granny,
so that when I'm dying
I will find my way back to
you, Scioto County.
I will find my way back to you.
We are household, we are family.

Push me in the river instead of
filled with formaldehyde,
hidden in fiberglass lined in satin,
mauve to match my cheeks.
May all alchemists live underground in
cemeteries full of
bodies turned to waves that can't break
free. Boil the water of us,
let nothing remain but scalding
steam, rising through air.

Enid, Called Granny

—1919

She's born to blossoming asters and goldenrod.
The war is over, the war is yet to come.

The Prayer No One Said at Her Birth

May that baby have steel in her veins,
so she'll walk by an X in the sand
knowing the bomb that's ticking can't
get her. Whatever shrapnel may come,
her lights are off and her blinds are down.
Just keep from her ears the insistent drip
of rain and leaky faucets loud.
May they never find her cracks,
may she never discover rust.

They'd Arrest You for That Now

—1936

Triumph or disaster the same to them, something to do in the season
after the haying was done but before the seeds were put in.
Elsie, the driver, would let them all tie their wood sleds to the back of his
bumper. He flung the wild boys from one side of the street to the other.
Grins on their faces and snow in their boots as the onlookers hooted and
hollered, they were towheaded kings of Main Street, adrenaline junkies
nothing to lose but an afternoon and their lives, which they thought a fair trade for a
moment of stardom, a flash of bright steel as they flew through the town.
But at the front of the bus there was one girl who paid them no mind, she sat
talking at length to the boy from the county home. No parents, no future,
past forgotten. Her father would flip his respectable lid if he
knew about this, if he knew of the way her mind whirled when the boy mentioned
anything found in the Song of Songs, especially lilies among the thorns,
especially bosoms and lips and bosoms and lips and (Oh!) lips.

The Boy from the County Home

—1936

The boy had come from up to Wheelersburg
a few years ago, at the start of the Depression times.
The crowded Scioto County Children's Home
had use for the girls who could cook and tend to things,
found space for the little ones that still cried in their beds
as visions of mothers and fathers unknown would play
in their heads when the lights had gone out and the night matron
    walked
through halls barely lit by small globe lights and slivers of moon.
Yet nothing could be spared for someone like him,
so close to a man, but still a boy by the law.
They'd let the teens go live at John Deaver's house
on the main street in Minford, close to the school and not far
from the farmers who'd pay for strong backs and quick hands
hungry for lives beyond hardscrabble hearts.

It Could Have Been Any Boy

—1936

Hello to the late spring sun
not yet so hot to crack the ground.

Hello to the seeds we've put away
from last year's pumpkin, squash, and beans,
those eaten and those left to the vine.

Hello to the boy with the godly voice
and eyes bright as willow's bark
hired for the season to lighten the load.

Hello to this heavy heart of mine
with its quick and secret beatings
with its cage of muscle and bone.

The Mosquito

—1936

The couple, that wasn't a couple,
rested beneath the green leaves
of the tulip poplar at the edge
of the front field of her father's farm.
There wasn't nothing tricky going on,
not to hear them tell it at least.
Just pals, that's all, just pals
working and laughing and praising the Lord.
The problem with shade is it calls the mosquitoes,
everyone wants out of the sun for a bit.
One landed itself on the strap
of her mud and sweat-caked overalls.
How long until it found its way
to some sweet spot of skin?

Enid Does the Work of Two

—1936

There were too many breaks,
Daddy had to let him go,
and now my body aches.

Hiring him was a mistake
though he could really hoe a row,
there were too many breaks.

Still easier than baking cakes
or learning how to sew,
but now my body aches.

Daddy said he couldn't abide snakes
when he saw him touch my elbow
plus, there were too many breaks.

"Relax," I said, "for goodness' sakes,
it wasn't as if he was my beau,"
and now my body aches.

I'm out in that field the moment I wake.
This is not how summer was supposed to go.
There were too many breaks
and now my body aches.

Scioto County Fair

—1936

Dete, whose real name was Janice,
said the way the French would say it,
heard the boys from the county home
got the *good* tickets to the fair:
ride all you want without a care.
All day, *all* night, Tilt-a-Whirl and
Ferris wheel for not even a penny.
Ishler, doing anything for
time with Enid, got an extra pair.
But she just *couldn't* be alone with him,
walked right by the carousel,
wouldn't abide the ups and downs of
things she couldn't control. Forget that
Ferris wheel, all lights and height,
forget the kiss at the end of the night.

Homecoming for the Ohio Council of Churches' Prince of Peace Declamation Contest Winner

—1936

She's glad to have him home
and wishes she had pearls to wear for him.
Small, smooth things on the strongest thread
a reminder that at the core of all beauty
is a hidden toughness holding it together.
They've come to be lifted along on his voice
to forget there's any land to be tilled
or plants to be staked. Nothing outside this
dark and expectant auditorium,
the rowdies and hecklers left at home for the night.
Nothing outside the echoes of his steps
as he takes the stage
light catching the bronze
of his Prince of Peace medal
all the way from Columbus
where he spoke so plain and clear
the city boys didn't stand a chance.

While Others Enjoyed the Beggars Night Ball

—1936

The bobbing for apples growing old
and not the kinds to tip a privy,
they left the school without a word
to walk along the gravel road.
He asked if she believed in ghosts
and could he shield her from the cold
of spirits passing in the night
and the devils lurking in men's souls.
Why no, she said with quick resolve,
I never have a thing to fear.
The Shadows? Empty as the tomb
when angels rolled the stone away.
He wanted to feel the warmth of her lips,
but settled for holding just one calloused hand.

Scenes from the Flood

I: First Date, *One in a Million* at the Columbia
    —*January 5, 1937*

Wet, but not too terribly so,
the couple that still weren't
a couple, settled into their seats
amid the rustle of coats
and newspapers, waiting sparks
catch the electricity between them.
Static or desire, who knows?
Don Ameche plays the part
of savior and wise man, witty
on the silver screen ahead
while crowds cheer a skating girl
fast on the slickness of the ice
knowing she'll come out of her spin
ready to do it again.

II: *Like Waiting on the Circus*
    —*January 18, 1937*

Waning to waxing, the moon
changed its light as the rain
kept coming down as before.
Children watched from the windows
of Lincoln School on the hill
hoping enough would show up
that class would be canceled,
that adventure would greet them
like a ringmaster waving
from the floodwall's top.

Famous flood wall
sixty some feet high,
those bricks and pumps
that made it safe
for little boys to take for granted
they'd grow to be big men.

III: Ding Dong Ditch
    —January 23, 1937

After all the alarms were long silent,
the water rang the doorbell
like a salesman come to call.
It was only a formality,
what with it already
coming up the stairs and all.
They opened the sewer drains
to let destruction rise
from below instead of crushing
everything from above,
but when it popped
the manhole covers off itself
they remembered loss is loss
no matter which way it hits you.

IV: Minford's Flood Stories Aren't Portsmouth's
    —January 23, 1937

Hollers kept safe by the hills,
not to mention the distance
between them and the river,
are misty and gray.

Does wander through with their fawns,
not yet worried enough
to seek higher ground.
If there's something to know,
they'll know in good time.
Warnings whispered by creeks and by runs
if their waters are fixing to
cover what little grass
there is to eat in the first place.
Deer are no fools, they'll listen.

V: Stories Not in the Documentaries
  —*January 24, 1937*

Prisoners shivered on the 3rd floor
of the emptied courthouse
shackled and waiting for transport
no one could say for sure
was ever coming.
What happened to the people
on the second floor
of the Negro American Legion
who hadn't anywhere
higher up to go
when the floor started buckling
and the building to collapse?

Cops were told
to shoot to kill
any looters they saw.
This is no time
for people like that.

Call into WPAY
for Christ's sake
and ask for help
like a civilized person.
You work together
or take your chances
with the river.

VI: The Only Death in Ohio Mothered
    One of the Few Black People
    Historians Ever Interview About the Flood
       —January 25, 1937

Bessie's gone under the water,
baby held high in the air
hoping that someone will grab her.
Safety was only a few streets away
when the boat capsized
into the flooded street.
Men in the nearby john boats
quickly plucked her boys out,
then reached for Bertie.
When they turned back for the mother,
fingers making contact,
second of hope split in pieces
as the Ohio made its claim.
Is it still the river
when it runs the muddy streets?
When it leaves its quiet banks
wandering in search of adventure?

VII: Heroes in All Sizes
   —*January 27, 1937*

Many people owe their lives
to teenage boys who got
fancy motorboats for Christmas
or National Guardsmen who said
If you don't get in this boat,
I will shoot you in the leg
and carry you down myself
when stubborn men wouldn't leave
their homes and their women
wouldn't leave them.
But how many people
owe their lives to little skinny
Albert Egbert shimmying through
the top floor window of Wurster's Drugs
to keep filling prescriptions
for people as long as he could
even if he'd never
seen them before that very second.

VIII: WPAY: We Play All Yodelers
   —*January 28, 1937*

No one listened to them,
that newer station that'd give
slots to people like the Morgan Boys
come in from the hollers
to sing a few songs late at night.

Keep them calls and postcards
coming in, folks! Fred Astaire,
Guy Lombardo, that's what
everybody wanted. Until
the water started coming down
and they had the sense to move
their transmitters upstairs.
Kept the lifelines open
calling from street to street.
A family needs food on 10th and Waller.
Two men on McConnell looking
for a ride to the mill
to pick up paychecks.
They promise they'll
help with the rowing.
Mrs. Simpson's at Mercy,
she's in perfect health
and wants you all to know
she's had a 7 lb boy.
Everybody loves you,
when you're singing their song.

IX: Second Date, Interrupted
    —January 29, 1937

Sightseers, don't park your cars
by the side of the road.
If you ain't here to help,
just get along home.

X: Third Date by the River
—*January 30, 1937*

Trains full of refugees
head to the north full of
children and dogs,
sickly sweet smell of
closeness and damp.
Columbus and Chillicothe
promise places for
5,000 souls.
Nothing can go south,
not over that river
no longer 2 miles wide,
but still not yet itself.
Enid wants to walk
the rail bridge to Kentucky,
see the current
through the slats,
dare it to take her on.
He stays in the truck,
watching her disappear
into the distance.

XI: *After All, the Water Will Come*
—*January 31, 1937*

Mud will harden to concrete
if left to settle there.

Everyone comes with brooms,
big push brooms meant
for you to put
your whole weight behind.
*When you focus
on action, fear
can find no foothold*
in the 2 inches of sludge
covering everything,
the 6,234 flooded houses,
the 34,248 homeless,
the 45,000 tons of debris,
the 16 million dollars of damage.
7 miles of new levee are built,
15 feet added to the flood wall.
Though it's not much more,
may it always be enough.
May we always be enough.

Best Behave Now

—1937

Lucille was hanging from the pipe beam
stretched along the shower wall,
naked as a jaybird, laughing
like a woodpecker in the fall.
Teammates hooted, egged her on,
save for one with a furrowed brow.
Enid, a downer since the flood, said
"Listen, you'd best behave yourself now."
But how she wished to swing there freely
right beside her rowdy friend.
How she wished to feel immortal
with those muscles Herculean,
ready for a dozen labors:
lions, hydras, her own dumb ticker.

If He Had Something

—1937

A bracelet of amber beads, a peck
on her expectant cheek.

> *If he had something to say to me,*
> *he should have said it plain.*

He told her she must listen close
to the song "Forsaken Love."

> *If he had something to say to me,*
> *he should have said it plain.*

While he went off to play soldier boy
she was left with games of chance.

> *If he had something to say to me,*
> *he should have said it plain.*

Just sitting at home with a radio
and static on the dial.

> *If he had something to say to me,*
> *he should have said it plain.*

Marcescence After First Love

—1938

The oak tree clings to dry, dead leaves
all through the winter months
and even now as spring comes on,
she will not let them go.

The Boy in the Dress Blues

—1939

He went to look for her
at her family's market stall.
Her sisters were selling that day,
their table full of treats
and trinkets, rusted nails
from when the old barn came down.
A jar of Queen Anne's lace jelly,
a summer's day preserved.
You never knew what someone would want.

Before he left he asked:
When would she be around?
and *Where was she right now?*
and *Was she doing well?*
"I expect she's with her husband,"
Dete said, acting like
she was just being helpful,
acting like she didn't know
the weight of her words on the boy.

How Easily She Broke the Thing

—1987

How easily she broke the thing,
a bracelet her granny let her wear,
just baubles on a string.

She snapped it to feel the sting,
a little fidgeter unaware
how easily she broke the thing.

They hit the wood floor with sharp pings.
The old woman said she didn't care,
just baubles on a string.

But her heart felt the sting
and her memory cracked like glassware.
How easily she broke the thing.

The boy couldn't afford a ring,
she gave no promises or swears,
just baubles on a string.

She'd found someone new by spring.
When he came home, he was unprepared
how easily she broke the thing,
just baubles on a string.

At the Tracy Park KIA-MIA Memorial

—1995

Sitting on stone that'd been quarried just down the road a piece,
hearing the gas station clerks with their young voices cracking
Go ahead pump seven. Go ahead pumps nine and two, her
hand reaches out to his name dug deep in the granite.
Fingers follow the curves of his *s*'s in ways that
memory pretends they once did in real life, and she wishes for
pencils or crayons to make an impression of him,
something to put in the scrapbook beside the clipping,
brittle but legible, the war had hardly even started.
The boys on the field in the distance keep going *Hut,
hut, hut,* as she breathes in the air of the evening.

The Husband

Confluence

—1933

Afternoon heat with mosquitoes in every small, shady spot,
she and Dete headed to swim where the creek meets the Little Scioto,
down by Bobwhite Hollow and out past old Wheeler's Millhouse.
Modest black swimsuits with no frills to speak of, they'd worked long and hard for the
store-bought contraptions with worsted wool and a mermaid-stamped tag.
Such an extravagance, weren't they so fancy, didn't their callouses
spark to the chill of the water as they giggled and splashed in their secret
world with the warblers and wrens their sweet stalwart companions and guardians.
But up around a subtle bend, those hot, ornery boys,
they were hopping in and, would you believe, were just naked as jays.
All dingles and dangles, with muscles ripe from the hogs and the hay.
They would swear later on that they had no idea that the girls were right there.
Just funning and sunning, a lark and a dare, not meaning to make
a show of themselves, not meaning to scare the birds all away.

She Sets Her Sights on the Next Bright Boy

—1937

Though he was the butcher's kin,
she found it hard to put aside
his playing fiddle and cards all day
instead of coming to the school.
She'd heard all about his mischiefs and pranks,
even seen one herself on a hot
summer day when her heart wanted more
or less to be left alone with itself.
But perhaps he had potential and charm
being one of the loud and well-loved boys,
being one of those who brought the sun
to the deepest holler's shade.
Perhaps he'd do her days some good,
perhaps he'd burn her inside out.

Another Beggars Night Ball

—1937

The boy who'd dropped out at fourteen
never making it past long division and graphs,
had charmed his way through the door and spiked
the punch with something cheap and potent
he'd stowed inside his overcoat.
Then, when he grew bored, he took her hand
and asked *Would you like to get out of this place?*
They put the rock inside the can
and left the can in the road, then hid
behind the privy watching cars
nearly miss the trick they'd played,
the smell and closeness rattling her nerves.
You know, they're just lucky no one got hurt.

A Winter Walk

—1938

Walking up the snowy hillside
with the moonlight shining on them
like a blessing from the heavens
like permission from the watching
deer among the oak and pine trees,
with the crunching, echoed footfalls
muffling all his nervous chatter,
LeRoy reached for her gloved hand.
But she pulled away discreetly,
almost like she hadn't noticed
what the boy was cooking up,
almost like she hadn't noticed
how his face flushed with each heartbeat,
how his breath kept making dream clouds.

Guard

—1938

She didn't see him along the wall,
her mind so taken with other things
like blocking the tall girl from Portsmouth High
or clearing a path on the court for Lucille;
like keeping the laces tied on her shoes
or staying in the good graces of Coach.
She didn't see him along the wall
refusing to sit with his friends or his kin.
If he sat it would wrinkle his suit and *then*
who would he be? Just some boy in the crowd
who'd dropped out of school and spelled think with an *a*?
Just a loafer, a crumb bum watching the game
no better nor worse than that goof that she ran
with before, who she thought of as just a good friend?

Natural Selection

—1938

I

Shumway girls love those playful boys
because they frolic like the deer.
The WPA gave his father land,
then sent the boys to put down roots.
In August, no crops were in the ground
and LeRoy sat and played the fiddle
while his brothers plucked their teeth.

II

If she is to be settled now,
let it not be to some silly boy,
some grinning, motorcycle boy,
some drinker of homemade hooch.
Let her take up hearth with a boy
who builds a fire, a porch where she rocks
their baby to sleep and sings while he
plants her corn and beans for next year.

III

or let her take up with no boy at all,
but a man who tries to understand.

Not Understanding Confinement,
She Doesn't See the Big Deal About Shoes

—1938

He had planted the fields in May
but by June, walked only in the meadows.

The bean seedlings pushed through solid clay
yet he cared only for the chicory and ironweed,

those wasteland flowers that took so little
care, gave so little back, so his father said.

When the woman visited, she brought the rains
and flooded the low spot at the back of the cabin,

filled the well again, walked the rows with lightning.
In the flashes, the corn rose up and the tomatoes reddened.

But he would not have her with feet muddied,
he would not have her with toenails long.

Her brothers, a wall of gray, stood beside her,
saying no man should pass.

But a week later, she went to Marting's
to pick up her patent leather 7 wides.

With their clean cotton laces and firm rubber soles,
she walked the roads back down the holler.

Chicken Fighting

—1939

Couples still with no children to speak of
splashed with the wives on the shoulders of husbands
balancing in youth and in summer's first rays
knowing that nothing could bring them to topple or
sway, and that foolishness always won out over
time clocks and whistles and clamoring bosses.
Skinks on a rock, they sunned themselves after
trapping the heat of the day in their heartbeats,
storing it busheled to bursting like peapods
greened and tough with the season's progressing.
Soon all their houses would fill up with worries
growing too fast for their pockets and purses,
pushing them farther away from the mill pond,
pulling them toward an unspeakable ocean.

Mother-in-Law as False Prophet

—1939

She prayed for flaky biscuits, browned
to perfection, hot and buttery,
a testament to her devotion
learned against her will. *A wife*
is only so good as her breakfast plate,
so best not burn the bacon rinds
and keep the coffee nice and strong,
your egg yolks set, not too hard or soft.
But when he woke, he smiled at her
and pulled her from the stovetop's heat,
a messy curl not yet combed back,
the stubble still left on his cheek,
I don't know as I'm quite hungry yet.
What do you say we go to bed a bit?

Window Shopping

—1940

The best seeds are the stolen ones that gather up lint
inside the pockets of plaid shorts or overalls,
the ones stripped from their stalks, hid without a hint
of mischievous wrongdoing or breaking of laws.
The best furniture comes from the side of the road
or foraged from the depths of the dump next door
and pulled to the house's safety before it rained or snowed,
before the late winter sun woke up the mold spores.
But, if she had that new dresser, at least new to her,
she would sand it and paint it and line all the drawers,
slip in a sachet of lavender, maybe some myrrh,
and then brag to her sisters about how it'd come from the store
with its little box on top for her colors and scents.
Now wouldn't that just be something, yeah, that sure'd be
    something!

That LeRoy Is Such a Card

—1943

When his brother asked if they'd named the baby yet:
No, we were thinking something more like Janice.

Priorities

—1944

letters are passing each other in transit

*Please, if you can't forget Sunday,
forgive me for it, will you?*

writing and sending at least one each morning

*Next time I'm home, I won't see nobody.
You and the girls, that's it. I promise.*

pages thin and full of misspellings

*Send me a box of King Edward cigars,
if you've got money, and still love me.*

Love Forever, LeRoy

—1944

She set the girls down in their chairs
and filled their bowls with Corn Flakes and milk,
too tired even for oats and eggs,
though she understood them to be
the healthier choice, and cheaper too,
with the chickens right next door and all.
She'd lie and tell him she'd fed them right.
Today, she just didn't have it in her.
While Jannie and Bunk were munching away,
content with whatever got put down before them,
she read the letter over again,
was glad to hear he liked the chow
they served in the mess hall, but tingled with
I sure do miss your biscuits, dear.

Platoon 339 Leaves Camp Lejeune
and Is One Step Closer to the Front

—1944

It was just a week ago tonight I kissed you
goodbye and now the whole country is between us.
I barely made it back in time. The sarge
was doing roll call, the first of many that day
to be sure not a one of us run off from camp.
Of course, some guys did, but they brought them back right quick
to stand beside the rest of us Marines
like worried, well-trained, fitful ducks in a row.
When I'm walking guard duty here at Camp Pendleton,
the moon at night is almost as bright as the day
and Honeybunch, I miss you something awful
when I think I might have to use all this stuff I've been taught.
If I don't ever see you again, don't feel bad about it,
for you were the swellest wife anyone ever had.

Sometimes Distraction Is the Only Hope There Is

—Jannie Lou, 1944

Tap dancing child without shoes or a reason,
Laugh at me. Smile for me. Show me you care for me,
listening to mother, who sews by machine now,
forcing herself through the piecings and stitchings.

Who Says That's Even What She's Looking For?

—1945

Someone would bring her the newspaper daily, its
easily torn pages and barely dry headlines.
Each day a list of who wouldn't be sending
any more letters or asking his girl to
buy him a bus ticket home for the holidays.
Each day a list of the boys from her class, or
just a little bit younger, who threw no more
pennies in deep wishing wells, no more hopes kissed in
zinc-coated steel for those futures so bright.
Oh, how her sisters would laugh at her ritual.
If something'd happened to LeRoy, she wouldn't be
finding it out from the *Portsmouth Times*.
Surely they'd telegraph, call, or stop by, silly
girl with your fingers all ink-stained and nailbeds all
caked in the dirt of yesterday's planting.

Quiet Secrets in Wartime

—1945

She can guess where he is, but not what he's done,
though really, she guesses at that as well.
He's told her enough of the socks wet with mud,
the darkness of caves, and the cheers, *like at ball
games up home,* as another man's brought to his death.
Her secrets seem small when compared to his.
The girls' hair left in rats for a week, sometimes more
while she helped plant the seeds in neat rows with her dad.
For a time, she was nobody's mother or wife.
She couldn't control the wind or the rain.
She couldn't control the price set for grain.
All she could do was dig up the land
good and soft, making sure all the rocks were moved out,
making sure all the roots had some space for themselves.

Traveling Light

—1945

These stories come from his letters to her,
safely stored in a green metal box
passed down to their son, my dad,
who scanned them and sent them around
through Gmail, Yahoo, and WOW,
so we all could have our own copies to keep,
so we all could enter these memories at will.
But her letters to him have been lost,
even those he kept safe in his gear
because they were especially lovely ones.
When the medics cut the straps off his pack
after he was rocked from the cliff,
they quickly tossed it all aside.
He was in no state to say *Wait!*

That LeRoy Is Such a Card II

—1945

When his commanding officer asked if he'd
let the enemy get away:
Well, no, he didn't get away,
but I sure 'nough did.

Packing Up

—1945

Carols still linger, stale in the air, while the
babies play with the blocks and a train set kept
under the tree. She is dancing around them,
putting the popcorn aside for the birds, wrapping
ornaments up for next year as one Santa Claus
face disappears in a shrouding of shoe ads and
pictures of men coming home to their women,
whispering stories blocked out by the censors.
Take down the tree before New Year's Day.
Months have gone by as they promised him safety,
promised him home, a way out of the Marines that
didn't involve a draped flag or a stretcher.
All that he asks for his homecoming welcome,
Please, don't remind me of all I have missed.

Homecoming

—Bunky, 1946

Bunk salutes her dad's returning
puts a cap upon her head and
dons a uniform her mother
sewed while keeping busy getting
no news from Pacific fronts.

Not Caring the Color of His Heart, She Tries to Raise the Dead

—1947

I

LeRoy lost his hearing in the war.
They told the children it was mortar fire,
so they wouldn't worry, would just accept
something far away and collateral,
not the grenade thrown right at him.
They told this lie like it mattered,
like the babies with their chubby arms
understood anything other than their father
felt like ash and artillery
instead of pipe smoke and cooked meats.

II

She handed him a fiddle, then a banjo with three strings.
She handed him a bowl of hot beans and a spoon,
but he just kept rocking on the porch
of their small house in the holler.
She put color on her lips, Vaseline on her lashes,
wore a dress cut so low it made her blush.
His rocking bent the boards, but didn't stop.

Not Understanding Palimpsests, My Grandmother Thinks She Can Leave the Holler

—1949

She had the will to rise
    from the shaded holler
        where spring peepers hid
            in the tangles of honeysuckle

to desert to its dust the road
    lined with tiger lilies
        and the mix and match leaves
            of the quick growing sassafras.

Look at her truck
    packed up with the babies
        and a used store-bought dresser,
            a special place for her colors and scents.

Watch how she keeps her back
    to the outhouse her own hands dug
        and the shack bought and paid
            with calloused hands and late nights.

This will be a summer place
    where the babies' babies' babies
        will salt potato salad and pour red
            Kool-Aid from large glass pitchers,

a place for them to say,
>   *We were once so country,*
>   before heading home to town
>   where real life traps you in aluminum

              siding, concrete walkways,

                  neighbors in

                          hailing distance

Through the Blades

—1950

It's what he wants, so it's what he'll get.
Not bologna on Wonder, chips and a Coke,
he wants bologna *salad,* bread
with no crust, a thermos of coffee, black,
with an apple, no matter the time of year.
Then biscuits and bacon at suppertime
because he isn't ready for them
before he knows what the day will bring.
But what she wouldn't give to get
a day without complexities,
a day without the whirl and cut
of taking a perfectly serviceable
piece of meat and blending it
beyond the laws of Christ and Man.

Bedtime Story

—1951

In the quiet of the night that comes
after every last *one last story*
after every last *one last glass of water,*
he tells her all his *I'll tell you one days.*
The thrill and zing of bullets missing
as he ran out to bring in supplies
tossed from airplanes to muddy fields
because the roads were too wet to be roads,
because to stop and think was to die.
He didn't think for over a year.
When he came back to himself
he gave the men in the brig extra sandwiches,
let them out for a picture show,
just so long as they promised
to return in one piece.

That LeRoy Is Such a Card III

—1952

When the children asked about his Purple Heart:
Don't you worry about me,
they just gave me this when I got stabbed
with a fork in the chow line one day.

Late Riser

—1954

Church bells in the distance,
the alarm is going off.
They'll be late again for sure,
if they make it there at all.

He was baptized in the South China Sea
right before they joined the fray.
If a little fear was what it took,
well, that was fine with her.

I'm a good boy now, I am.
I've found the Lord, or rather,
he found me I s'pose.
If I get home, you'll see.

Church bells in the distance,
the alarm is going off.
They'll be late again for sure,
if they make it there at all.

He made promises to the ocean,
like Wimpy with his burgers,
"I'll gladly pay you Sunday
for a Psalm 91 today."

The Sunshine Church of Christ
prayed for him each day
after the Chaplain's letter.
He finally was worth saving.

Church bells in the distance,
the alarm is going off.
They'll be late again for sure,
if they make it there at all.

Mama Says, If the Cancer Don't Kill Him, She Just Might

—1957

Cold as the stone that is not yet a statue,
children play coatless in the thin line of willows,
dreaming of days running barefoot on fescue.

Mother is watching while prepping the stew,
dicing the carrots and peeling tomatoes,
cold as the stone that is not yet a statue.

Father's a rattling ruckus, kazoo
playing along with the song on the radio,
just like a wild child running through fescue.

Last month, he brought home some bagpipes, tried and true
star of his concrete-floor-basement variety show.
His breath like a stone, he is not yet a statue, not

yet a fogged memory of a man who
laughed with a hearty, life-giving staccato
bursting with days running barefoot on fescue.

Yesterday's treatments—his skin thin as tissue—
no assured protection against a tomorrow
cold as the stone that is not yet a statue,
far from the days running barefoot on fescue.

That LeRoy Is Such a Card IV

—1957

When his wife asked about the future:
Well, I just hope your next husband treats you right.

All the Wild Things Kept Inside

—1957

A duck and a dog
and a groundhog too,
all the muddy footprints
left on her clean floor.
When he has gone,
there will be peace.
No more beagles
brought in off the street,
no more whistling at dawn and dusk.
And she will plug
the gap in the bedroom floor
where Sir Chuckling has chipped his way
from his burrow below.
When he is gone
she will look down
into that hole and yell,
"Stay out, you fool,"
or perhaps, she will crawl her way
into the darkness with him.

The Widow's Yoga

—1957

They say she stood on her head,
stayed like that for days
letting her man wash out
through the crown to the earth.

They say that when she came down
she cooked beans and cornbread salted
with her own tears, which the kids
ate of heartily.

Not Her Husband All Safe in His Grave

—1958

She wanted a place where stitches all stayed stitched
and the milk jug was always full in the fridge,
where the older girls didn't stop at the corner store
on their way home from school to buy candy bars
telling the clerk to just put them on credit,
where no one snuck out to the hop or drove halfway to the moon.

She wanted the girls, who she thought hung the moon,
to think less about keeping their brother in stitches
or watching *Roy Rogers* clear through to the credits
and more about the spilled milk in the fridge,
the wildly swinging front gate they'd forgotten to bar,
the list of small things they'd promised to get at the store.

What would their futures have in store,
with their pale city calves bright and white like the moon
and their skin soft and clean from Dove soap bars
sudsed up on washcloths with pulled stitches,
night cream kept fresh on a shelf in the fridge?
Depending on how they turned out, she'd take the credit,

but not the pointy hot poker of blame, only the credit,
which she'd keep in her heart like a dragon's store
all glistening gold. Of course she'd clean up the fridge,
to leave it would be like tide fighting moon,
because Mother Nature hasn't so much stitched
them together as boiled them hot and made metal bars.

And what can you buy with the gold bars
of housework and keeping, done without credit,
of pink party dresses and majorette uniforms stitched
on her Singer because to buy from the store
was as unthinkable as reaching the skin of the moon,
as elusive as a fully stocked fridge?

Who else would clean the spill in the fridge?
Not the boy in his shirt with the red and white bars,
not the baby in her romper covered with stars and with moons,
not the teenagers with their jejune views on credit,
not the clerk down at Uncle Raymond's store,
only her between the ironing and hems that needed stitched.

At night the hum of the fridge sings a song to her credit,
its electric eight-bar melody shakes, but can't take, the store
of bright moon dust held to her soul, good and stitched.

Enid,
Herself

She Knows What Counts

—1962

Five years have passed since her man has died
and she has been so good;
watching the children and keeping them clean
as pennies in a jar.

Four children need an awful lot
of cornbread, beans, and milk.
The Mill and Marines give their due,
but it's never quite enough.

Three men make eyes at LeRoy's wife
(that's what she'll always be)
but when she dares return a glance,
the past is all she sees.

Too many people talk in town
(and talk and talk and talk).
She has no space to think them through,
these matters of the heart.

One gossiped bit of kiss and tell,
one man where he shouldn't be
then the neighbors, they'll have much to say.
She'll tell herself, *Of course they're right.*

The Widow Takes a New Beau

—1964

Hidden behind the wisteria,
cuddled against the cold darkness . . .
No, it's not fair to say cold.
Chilly, it is just a bit chilly.
June is still thinking of summer, though
hasn't yet made the commitment to
warm, sweaty evenings refusing the
needed release of the day's heat.
Yet she is not like the winter or
even the spring with its snows coming
late and unexpectedly expected.
Where do we put her then? With her
shorts and her sweater together?
Here, on the swing with her eyes gently
closed to the grace of the evening.

Losing It

—John, 1966

Fresh PB&Js, a full encyclopedia set
with all day to read as the rain hit the tin of the roof above,
his two older sisters shaking their heads at him reading the world
like a novel and not the disjointed histories and facts of the truth.
He'll remember the act, but nothing he read and he'll wonder aloud
how he lost all the things that he knew at seven. Where had it
    gone?
Where was the rise of the British Empire? Where was the fall
of Byzantium? Where were the cases of Adler and Freud?
They were lost in Southern Hills, in the crackle of shock
treatments and meds and forcing himself to be real.
Maybe it fused him together and maybe it shattered him more
until he felt glowing like a Renaissance saint, like a star
and not just one more Thorazine script, one more real gone kid
with all of him broken to bits, no one winning but Smith, Kline,
    and French.

Hot Bath After Someone Else's Breakdown

—1967

She closes the door on the noise of the house and begins to soak
in the warm water with its rosy scent of Dove.
After she's clean, she'll begin to get ready for her date.
The sound of her not-yet-teen still carries through. Her talk
is louder than the door is thick. She's listing the faults,
to a friend on the phone, of every boy for miles around.

The dump is gone, they're building houses all around
her now. The change is almost too much for her to soak
in, so lately she's been neighborly to a fault
and cooing at the new women like some kind of dove
inviting them over for tea, an afternoon of talk,
though few of them have taken her up on it to date.

She doesn't know where they are going on their date.
She guesses dinner, then perhaps they'll just wander around
and take a moment to forget the chitter and talk.
The way they were acting, you'd think she was getting sloshed and soaked,
instead of just stepping out with this man, this gentle dove,
(okay, well he has a bit of a temper, his only fault).

Last year, when her boy took sick, they said it was all her fault.
Her sisters sniped, *he was fine until you began to date.*
How can you show such disrespect to LeRoy? Doves
still mourn him, why don't you? Don't you miss him around?
What right had they to treat her that way? Her soul felt soaked
in sour milk, even by Effie, who had no room to talk,

seeing as it was her who just about had talked
her into it in the first place. No one should fault
a woman for living her life, for trying her best to soak
up the rays of a dying day with a few little dates
after so many years. It wasn't like she was running around
or bathing herself in Shalimar instead of Dove.

It wasn't even soap. The wrapper said it was Dove
"Beauty Bar," which, okay, was probably New York talk
for fancy soap, but still, it was innocence all around
her in the steamy bathroom air with no one at fault
and no one yammering away with all those out-of-date
notions that get in the way of a widow just having a soak.

Olive branches, doves, it was no one's fault.
Let the others talk and rattle, she's got a date,
her life's not bound by their silly bilge and soak.

Our Lord and Savior 4-F

—John, 1970

God bless the times of arts and crafts, the peace
he found as delicate wood was bent and shaped.
His friends were sending letters home from the heat,
the war in the jungle they rejected him from.
They couldn't trust him with guns. Couldn't trust
the aim of a boy like that, a mixed-up, wild boy.
Small blessings, safely tucked away, top floor,
Scioto County Receiving Hospital.
Instead of dog tags, he has these relics—
a Picasso replica becoming unglued,
the grains of sand that fall away from the board
revealing the plywood beneath. And every day
the dulcimer made of pine is showing cracks
in cheap black and yellow latex-painted sides.

It Wouldn't Have Changed a Thing

—1982

As he sits in the red chair dying,
she is thinking how it would have been
different if she'd ever said *yes*.
Paramedics are already there,
though it's probably too late.

Would she have kept him from the pain
if that night at the Johnda Lou Drive-In,
hot and bothered from the weather and
Lady Godiva Rides Again,
her answer had been *yes* or

if after that almost perfect day
walking the paths in Shawnee Forest
crunching leaves so red and yellow or

if after eating chili dogs
at the A&W stand or

if after his first heart attack or

if drinking sweet tea on the porch or

if after his second heart attack or

or or or or
if after if after if after
or if or if or if or . . . if.

If It Ain't Broke

—1984

They hung the laundry together
on the line between their houses:
underwear and rayon bras,
polyester blouses.

One still used a wringer,
pushing clothes through with a stick,
and even though she sweated,
This don't bother me one bit.

She said it helped her to remember
the cost of living life,
the work it takes to undo
the body's mess and strife.

Quit your fooling, said the other,
I won't hear one more peep.
Don't be so high and mighty,
we all know you're just too cheap.

A Visit to Spalding County, Georgia

—1984

Dete has long ago left the river,
left the woods and market stalls too.

Girls who played in concrete basements,
grown to women off to desk jobs

children of their own to tend to
grateful for an aunt's short visit.

Quilts and canning, cakes and cleaning;
house that's turning back in time.

Once it's all to rights, she wanders
through their small suburban forest

really just a stand of poplars,
southern red oaks, a few sweetgums.

Enid sees the kudzu growing,
gets a knife from out the kitchen.

When the eldest returns that evening,
there's a basket full of apples

woven from the nuisance vines:
beautiful and stable, her monument.

All the Women in My Family Have Singers But Me

—1985

We sat on the covered porch,
not screened in, just covered,
and watched the rain come down.

Reading our papers and books,
eating meat sandwiches with tea,
so sweet and straight from the fridge.

She'd tried to teach me to sew
earlier in the day. Machine sew,
really sew. I was already
quite good with my hands.

Don't be afraid now, she said
when she saw me hesitate
at the ups and downs of the needle,
everyone runs it through
their hand on accident at some point.
Ain't no big deal.

Which was meant to comfort me,
but only made things worse,
as is so often the case
when we tell each other such things.

Best Behave Now II

—1988

There once was a woman from Scioto
who rode to church in a Toyota.
With her best frenemy,
she gossiped with glee
and prayed that the Lord would forgive her.

First Thanksgiving After Renovations

—1990

All the boot camps and high school commencements collide,
they slide whopper-jawed on the second shelf
of the blue weathered hutch that's almost built-in,
all these pictures she's moved to make space for the punch.
In that crystal bowl on the barrel sits
a mixture of Kool-Aid and Sprite. It's caught
the gray dust that's shaken free from the grate.

The prized bowl is just a detergent reward,
a cut-glass reminder of water and heat
bought with loads of laundry and box tops she'd saved.
Everyone who shows up remarks
on how the door is not where it ought
to be according to the plan;
how the space above the ceiling fan leaks;
how she should have listened to Lucille
and not let the contractors charge her for more
than the grant from the village would let her afford.

Who cares? She's bored of the topic real quick
and heads to the kitchen with its new
pass-through to the dining room,
a way for her to keep up on the talk
while still watching the turkey, slicing the veggies,
whisking the gravy as much as she likes
(which isn't particularly much),
pretending this work is urgent
and not just a way to escape from us all.

People Should Be at Home When It Rains

—1998

They baited the bear on Harrisonville
with doughnuts from the Crispie Creme, to lure
it back to the woods where it belonged,
away from the dump, away from Granny's
kitchen window and small gardens.

With what do they bait
the widow away
from these milltown blues?

A trail of carp through the Appalachians
until she finds herself near the sea, feels
that she should stay? But no one's leading her,
they know her sunshine pleases, never talk
about the clouds. And if her floods
should catch them unaware and dreaming,
lost in the beauties of her dark eyes
and smooth skin, she won't feel sorry
as her inland tides pull them out.
Any fool could've read the forecast.

Hey There, Hornworm, Hawkmoth,
or Whoever You Are

—2003

In a yard that smelled of mint and marigolds
her vegetables grew by the wall of bricks
salvaged one by one from the dump next door.
She thought it'd take the child all day,
not counting on his Campbellite soul and Radio Flyer wagon.
Walking the row, her touch of each plant's leaves
looked like a moment of transcendence,
but she merely checked for damage.

Knowing every hornworm eventually finds itself
blending with the backs of elms,
a beauty not worth risking
her Best Boys and Early Wonders for,
she picks them off.

She would have sacrificed if they were rosy maples,
or the woolly bears with their stripes telling
of the winter to come. But not these,
oh not these who will only grow
into a master of disguise that does not know
who it really is, oh, not these.

Granny at the Gallia Street Golden Corral

—2005

Let her wear the straw hat with fake flowers.
Let her wear her good set of sneakers.
Let her wear the pink pearl necklace.
Let her wear her maroon sweatshirt.

Can you tell her it's not at all
what she hopes, what she imagines;
that the lights are just fluorescent,
plates and trays are rough brown plastic?

When she looks around the restaurant,
surveying the folks living common li(v)es,
will you tell her she is special?
Will you act like you don't know?

Granny, Called Enid

—2006

No one has heard a peep from her since Monday.
Everyone knows she's just with someone, somewhere.

Gathering aster seeds out to Bunky's,
hunting buckeyes to string a holiday wreath,

visiting Zel or her kin in the holler.
Next door neighbors estimate Tuesday evening.

Dried leaves collect in the cracks of her doorway.
Feral cat on the porch's been going hungry.

When her children find her, she will be nothing
but an empty skin in the shape of a poem.

Notes

Historical information on the Ohio River Flood of 1937 is taken from *New York Times* articles. Interviews with Alberta Parker and Lettie Clark available on the Scioto County Library YouTube channel and Nathan Lorentz's 2002 documentary *River Voices* were invaluable resources while writing "Scenes from the Flood." Italicized phrases in the poem come from these interviews, most notably, the phrase "after all, the river will come," which is from Rose Jacobs.

Poems about WWII draw heavily from the letters of LeRoy Schomburg to his wife Enid. Italicized lines are direct quotes from his letters.

The Minford Local Schools website's local history archive was an incredibly helpful tool for me in creating this story.

The phrase "they know her sunshine pleases" in "People Should Be at Home When It Rains" is based on the line "I know my sunshine pleases" from Emily Brontë's poem "Shall earth no more inspire thee."

About the Author

Jennifer Schomburg Kanke, originally from Ohio, currently lives in Florida. Her work has recently appeared in *New Ohio Review, Massachusetts Review, Shenandoah,* and *Salamander.* She is the winner of a Sheila-Na-Gig Editions Editor's Choice Award for Fiction. Her zine about her experiences undergoing chemotherapy for ovarian cancer, *Fine, Considering,* is available from Rinky Dink Press (2019). She can be found online hosting the writing podcast *Meter&Mayhem.*